The Reverend Derek Nuttall MBE was a URC Minister and National Director of the bereavement charity Cruse. He played a vital role in helping the village of Aberfan, South Wales, recover from the tragedy of October 1966, when a coal mining waste tip slid onto their school and killed 116 children and 28 adults. He was a devoted family man who married twice: first to Margaret, with whom he had three children, and then to Doreen after Margaret's early death. He had four grandchildren who enjoy his passion for storytelling.

In memory of Derek, dad, granddad and all he loved in life.

Derek Nuttall

POEMS OF LIFE AND LOVE

AUSTIN MACAULEY PUBLISHERS™
LONDON * CAMBRIDGE * NEW YORK * SHARJAH

Copyright © Derek Nuttall 2024

The right of Derek Nuttall to be identified as author of this work has been asserted by the author in accordance with sections 77 and 78 of the Copyright, Designs and Patents Act 1988.

All rights reserved. No part of this publication may be reproduced, stored in a retrieval system, or transmitted in any form or by any means, electronic, mechanical, photocopying, recording, or otherwise, without the prior permission of the publishers.

Any person who commits any unauthorised act in relation to this publication may be liable to criminal prosecution and civil claims for damages.

A CIP catalogue record for this title is available from the British Library.

ISBN 9781035817092 (Paperback)
ISBN 9781035817108 (ePub e-book)

www.austinmacauley.com

First Published 2024
Austin Macauley Publishers Ltd®
1 Canada Square
Canary Wharf
London
E14 5AA

Thank you to Doreen Nuttall for her patience in typing out the poems and bringing them to the attention of the publishers.

When Will I Love You?

I will love you then, when
Tides have no more ebb and flow,
When sun's light and moon's glow
Have lit their last dawn and dark,
When time ticks no more;
I will love you then, when
All is clear and eternal secrets
Are revealed, when pain is at an end,
And peace pulls all together;
I will love you then,
When the heaven we know is known
By all, when our love blossoms
Full and rich, in that eternal place,
I will love you then, then begin
Again, to love you more.

Welcome Back

Welcome back my love,
Welcome back
To arms that long to hold you,
Hands that thrill to touch you,
Lips that long to speak your name.

Welcome back my love,
Welcome back,
With a kiss that's born for you,
A smile reserved for you,
A longing stirred by you.

Welcome back my love,
Welcome back
To a heart that beats for you,
A life that's lived for you,
A soul that mates with yours.

Welcome back!

Valentine's Day

O Sainted Day,
Whose innumerable hours—
Since Valentine gave Name—
Have echoed with love's telling,

Tremulous first-offered love,
Brave love of unconquerable spirits,
Love in moist-misted eye, in awed
Hands, in later, tender age,
Love in gifted rose, scented card,
In silent adoring,
Love from distance, hoping,
All loves you have known.

O Sainted Day, you who have heard
So much, what more is there to speak?
This, this, hear this, hear of our love,
Love that in the telling grows, that helps
Bear the unbearable time when
We're apart, that with radiance
Unmatched more than glimpses of heaven
But knows residing there, joy deeper
Than measuring,
Love, our love, that puts all
Love's pairings of the ages in its shade.
I may borrow from those who've
Graced your day, whose words
In every memory lies, yet they only
Half convey this love—
Infinity is too short a span to tell
It,
All other loves—moon to our sun,
Overture to our symphony, bud to our
Flower.

O Sainted Day, your hours will
Close, but no sun sets on our love, nor
Ever will,
It outlasts the fading day,
Outshines all lights, outbids
All other loves for favours of eternity,
O Sainted Day, be not wearied by
This love, for which
All that time ago, you were made.

To Stratford-On-Avon

As you travel to Stratford Town
'Long ribboned way,
And tree lined road,
Between the flickering slides
Of windowed scenes,
May our eyes together see,
And the journey share.

North of Oxford Town,
Blenheim's walled estate,
Round Palace proud,
Woodstock's charm,
Shipton's square, half hidden,
And Church tower's soar above
Tredington's honeyed stone.

And when in Stratford Town,
The river gay with
Wandering craft.
The peopled green,
The theatre, square behind,
Cottages, echoing past times,
And Holy Trinity, quiet, upstream.

And when back in London Town,
Keep within the remembering heart,
The thought,
The knowing,
That though on different days,
I saw and trod these ways,
I see them now with you.

To Northward Go

Would that I could northward go,
High above the ribboned roads,
O'er cloud-stained hills and
Fields marked clear by hedge and stone,

Would that I could northward go,
To the land of burn and brae,
Of purple heathered hills, and,
Lone piper's lament at dusk.

Would that I could northward go
To Moray's jagged coast,
To hear the sound of sea at dawn,
The gull's cry over harbour wall.

Would that I could northward go,
To walk with my love through the quiet ways,
And share the peace of the long, long day,
And the spell of the twilight hours.

Would that I could northward go.

To Love Like This

To love like this,
To be loved like this,
Is to be born,
Is discover the far range,
Deep seas, high tops
Rarely encountered in life 'til now;
Unbelieved if told by others,
Not dimly sensed as possible,
For love's reality strides beyond
Any fantasy or edge-of-sleeping dream,
It is to see what lay unseen
Through eyes baptised by all
Enfolding love,
It is an ever-widening way
To that eternity that is both
Cradle and destination of love.

There Is a Void

There is silence without you—
Sounds there may be, sounds there are,
But if it is not your voice, from
Close, our heads and hearts together, or
brought softly to the ear, in miracle way,
From across the miles,
There is a silence—
Not quiet, for that can be comforting,
But the silence of absence.

There is a void without you—
Things to do and diary needs to
Meet, but they are only attendants
To the occasion, preface to the words
That matter most, mere overture
To the melody, outer circles to the
Core of life
Which moves with you,
Void—not space which can be
Virginal for our creating, but
The void of emptiness.

There is loneliness without you—
Anonymous, or knowing, crowds
There may be, but without you
Near, within the hand's reach, or the
Distance of our love's smile, there is
Loneliness,
Not solitude, which can be peaceful,
But the loneliness of
Undiminished aching.

The Things I Know

These things I know—
With no doubt's shadow—
I could gaze at you
'Til all light dimmed,
And with each look
Be captivated anew.
I could spend all moments
With you
'Til time itself ends,
And know in tear and smile,
Unending, ever deepening joy.
I could hold you
'Til all strength ebbs,
And know with each embrace
Deeper oneness,
Contented peace.

The things I know,
With no wavering thought—
A night needs day
As ocean needs river, So I need you.
I yearn
And will yearn, for you,
'Til all and every passion ceases.
I love you
And will love you,
'Til earth and sun,
Moon and seasons
Fail to turn to nature's beat,
And I will always forever,
In whispered shapes,
Welling from that deep place
Where language itself is
Not yet formed.
Say—I love you

The Closing of the Day

Dusk is closing the
Eyelids of the day,
Hurrying clouds,
Pursued by a western wind,
Race for the shelter of the night,
And evening comes.

The river slows as
eyes no longer see its pace
Hills turn grey and soft,
And then are gone,
The reluctant sun gives ground
To rising moon,
And the day ends.
Each day has about it
Beauty and sense,
Save to it alone, that
No past can match,
No future quite repeat
Leaving memories,
Bookmarks in the tale of time.

This day my love
Has timeless bliss,
That fading memory
Will never steal away,
Such bliss that makes both
Heart and soul to soar
And words to falter in their forming.

Such bliss that brought
To birth a melody,
Not sung before,
A oneness dreamed,
And now made real,
A depth, unknown,
So lovingly shared.

The day closes,
And in solitary silence,
A prayer takes shape,
A tear breaks free,
A hand stretches across
The night dark hours,
And your firm hold is felt.

Tears Came

Tears came,
I could not contain them,
As I cannot contain my love for you,
They came as tidal waters raced
To compelling pull, and broke
Like rose and flower
Like poem and gift,
Symbol, taken, of ever deeper
Well,
Desiring your touch to come
And fill again
They came,

Tears of eye
And surging stream,
As end to precious time,
When loveliness anchored
My adoring look and nothing
Tamed the gaze.
When lighter, and deeper words,
Proved companionship,
When sweet rose
Presided over every touch,
Every meet of eyes
Every brush of beckoning lips
When linked hearts
And the corner of the universe
Knew only love.
They came
Those representatives of the heart,
As rose returned to earth,
As private paths
Widened to the roads of our other
Close times
And we knew again
The sweet, the painful—parting.

Saint Valentine

Ancient Saint, you did not know
What lay beyond your time;
A Day, engraved in special place,
Halfway through winter month,
Warming all who love,
And bringing early spring.

You could not have guessed
At how, in mischievous youth,
Cards, anonymous and
Slyly sent, would bring sudden flush
To pale face,
And mysterious urgency
Unfelt before.

You could not have foretold
Red rose gifts, poems toiled over,
'Times' pages scanned,
Romantic meals
And shy beginnings to
Life-long love;
You could not have seen.
How all sweethearts

Would feel young
On this Day, called by your
Ancient name as they know
The timelessness
Of love again.

Prescription in Colour

Sunshine gold

Moonlit soft silver

Rippling water white

Evening gentle green

Mix them when needed.

Autumn mist grey

Night deep blue

Velvet touch peach

Dusted damson purple

Take in as required.

On Sunday I Thought of You

I thought of you so much
In moments between the minutes,
In the silence between the sounds,
I thought of you.

I thought of you so much,
As pale sun ghosted
Through morning mist
As church folk gathered,
As bread was taken,
As wine was drunk,
I thought of you.

I thought of you so much
About routine tasks,
In restful pose,
No time all day
When I did not think of you.

I thought of you so much,
As Sunday closed,
As Monday began,
I thought of you.
I thought of you so much,
I pined for you so much.

Nature Seemed to Know

The full bloom of a rose
Wept, the night's tears still
On her velvet cheeks;
A green bush sobbed in the wind;
Clouds slid fast across the
Sky, restless;
The sun came and went
Not wanting to look for long;
Birds sang short,
Out of tune;
Twilight lingered mockingly,
And dawn crept so slowly
Into view;
And cruel time seemed not to care.

I Want to Walk That Way Again

I want to walk that way again
By hushed water, fed by
It's perceptible flow from
Tangled heights,
By falling stream, white
In its tumbling, and by foul
And flock, waiting for the
Artist's canvas of eternity;

I want to walk that way again,
By ancient buildings, bent with time,
Neighbours in their stories,
An age recalled, yet never to
Be recovered save in the imaginings;

I want to walk that way again,
Through arched stone,
Hear the centuries of devotion speak from
Rough-hewn and polished slab,
And pilgrim's lost moments,
To short-span bridge and
Threading path, intimate in dimension.
I want to walk that way again,

Where robins dart across the path,
Where hooves thud on bridle way,
Where nature is unharmed,
And innocent young play country games.
I want to walk that way again,
Where autumn tunnels through,
The wood, where water rises,
Smiles and disappears, where
Stretching roots hold back the
Banks, where fire smoke mists the trees.

I want to walk that way again,
Perpetually, no matter where
My tread, at one, as one,
My love and I, and
All of nature smiling.

I Love You

Your radiance shone
In the sunlit morning,
Your beauty,
Had no rival in nature's scene,
Your nearness
Tender
Alive
Your touch
Gentle
Thrilling,
Your kiss
Pure sweetness
Compelling passion
You,
In all your loveliness,
I love you

I Looked for You

I looked for you
In crowded store,
In busy street,
Looked at a thousand faces,
But none was yours.

I listened for you
Amid a thousand voices,
Among laughing groups,
Listened to every sound,
But your soft voice was not among them.

Yet I saw you,
And yes, I heard you,
Because I thought of you,
And you were there

I Need You

I have no home but
Beside you,
No peace,
Save near you
No rest but that
Found within your arms,
No rising thrill,
Save what you arouse,
No life, but what
You give birth to.

Fingerprint of Love

There's so much in touch—
Brief encounter of the marvellous kind!
Caress of stirring breeze,
Lap of soothing water
Conduit from fingertip to heart.
Stream surging into ocean
Threshold of passion.
Oasis of reassurance,
Channel of unspoken, unspeakable feelings.
Carrier of message "I'm here"
Fingerprint of love.

Come Muse

Come muse,
Come mantle of musicians,
Craft of the artist,
Sculptor's eye,
Come creations fullest power'
Give me all you have
To express such love,
Such beautiful love.

Come all marvellous music,
All lovers' rhymes
All nature's scenes before
Lovers' gaze.
Blend for me to
Show and tell my love.

Come gentleness of love,
Come surging passion,
Soul's oneness,
Heart's harmony,
Wondrous fusion,
Give me all you have
For me to give my love.
Come gay spirit,
Bright laughter,
Song on lips,
Dancing heart,
Come melodies of others,
Melodies we make ourselves.
Come deep,
Respond to deep,
Give me all I need,
To tell, to show, my love
Then give me more.

Book Marks in the Tales of Time

Scotney, a castle, time mellowed,
Quiet air alive with love,
Of past and forming,
Ever beckoning place.

A slow streams water,
Bumping its head on a low bridge,
Many alcove shop,
Misty Surrey Hills.

High arched bridge,
With London all around,
Yet only us, transfixed
By sights and sounds.

Still … by altar rail
In ancient church
Intimate, warm, dim light,
And flower-scented aisle.

A historic building's
Stretching acres,
Yet a corner of the world
To ourselves, and on time,
Concorde's waves split the sky.

Morning coffee in gracious places,
Genteel pinks, deep seats,
Fingers of columned marble,
Flowers in art-framed shapes.

Great art, each bound in by its frame,
Yet the beauty freed for watchers' eyes,
Gallery's guardians still
As the portraits around them.

A remembered village,
Shining in the rain,
Nothing yet open
Save one cosy place.

Woods and paths
In many places,
And summer's sun bright
Above a roof of leaves.

An Outdoor Performance

It took but a moment of Mozartian magic,
For centuries to drop away and
Common bush and balustrade and
Sun-firmed grass, to become
Spain,
Nature was audience too, trees so
Still in their listening, and night
Coming to look, too slowly to
Be seen, until in spotlights
Clever colouring, we were in a distant age;
And a tale unfolded, clear
To the ear and eye, loss and love,
Remorse and revenge, cunning and
Comedy, passion and punishment
So seriously funny, so
Funnily serious!
And another magic was abroad,
The page of another story penned,
Lovely music was drawn from
Within our hearts to fill that
Warm bowl of night;
My love,
Upon this stage of earth, aeons
Old, and familiar with stories,
No man has longed as deep
As I, nor more sought to
Find words to speak, not
Fabled tale, but true, true
Love.

A Greeting

A greeting to release the day

A link over the gulf of time

A fusion of heartbeats

A brush of angels' wings

A volume of words

A physical poem

A waterfall's cascade

A ripple of lightening

A magnetic homing

A sip of deep water

An instant symphony

And still indescribable!

A kiss

A Journey

Gleaming,
Wet with soft rain from
Deep dull cloud,
Masking any star or moon.
The necklace of lights,
Curving westwards
Away,
Away from you,
From you who give purpose
To journeys
Without whom achievement
Would be empty,
Success holds no meaning,
Discovery no joy in the telling,
From you
Whose company I crave
Above all else,
From you
You who have for all time,
And all eternity
My heart, my life,
My all,
Never to be withheld;
And now I sit,
In this still house,
No sound,
Out or in,
Longing for another journey
Soon, to your side,
To your arms,
To you
Source and destination of
My love,
For now, bed it must be,
To sleep away hours
That stand as barrier
Between us.

Your Love

Your love—

Is as spring in winter time

Rain on parched earth

Breeze in dormant sail

Word on blank page

Colour in dull landscape

Flower in desert place

Sun's ray in mist

Harbour in storm

Melody in silence

Peace in noise

Pulse in heartbeat.

'YES'
The YES on my lips,

Is the YES of my mind,

The YES in my eyes,

Is the YES of my soul,

The YES in my kiss,

Is the YES of my heart,

And the YES of my love,

Is the YES of my life.

When Do I Love You?

I love you each moment of each
Minute of each day, I love you
With each season's turn, each fall
Of night, each rising light;
I love you with each memory,
Each hope, each word, each look
Each thought, and touch and smile;
I love you in my solitude, and
In the together time,
I love you among the splendid grace, in
The simple place, before
Genius's art, and nature's changing
Gallery.
I love you in the
Meeting and the parting, in the beat
Of passion, in the still and quiet;
I love you in the many words, and in
The silent kiss, for
Which no words are made,
I love you and love you more.

When Did I Love You?

I loved you then, when the sun
First bronzed the sky,
When tears first fell from lowering
Cloud, when ice parted for a
Flower's birth;
I loved you then, when first words
Wooed the heart, when emotion,
Unknown before, stirred, when
Song was born;
I loved you then, when green first
Touched the barren soil, when
First a wave smoothed a distant,
Waiting, shore;
I loved you then, when Eden as
Still a distant dream, when
Love was conceived and lay,
pregnant,
In its mystery;
I loved you then, when sounds
Became poems, when timorous
Fingers touched and true life began;
I loved you then.

Waiting

I have a chariot waiting,
Poised for special places,
Our places,
Some known before, others awaiting
Our touch,
Places that will ever echo to our
Love.

I have a heart waiting
Expanding with each moment,
To give more, receive more, love,
A heart that has been changed by you and
Knows now no bounds.

I have a soul waiting,
Enriched by its meeting with yours,
To share all depths and heights.

I have more words waiting
To be given birth by you,
Given new colour by you.
I have a chariot waiting,
Where next my love?

Valentine's Eve

Eve of lovers' day.
Cupid's bow, stretched again
To lose life-changing shaft
To some expectant,
Some unknowing hearts.

Saint of love,
Give wing to gentle words,
Let them fly again to that
Heart that is both source
And receiver of my fond love.

Let not this eve,
Nor tomorrow's dawn
Nor any day
Without she knows,
In unconscious depth
Or fond recall,
My heart is hers.

Too Much ...

Time, you ask too much of me,
As hour by hour so slowly move,
You bid me patient, silent, be,
And heed not all my longing
For my love.

Sun-bright day you ask too much,
As woods and hills lie beckoning,
You want of me still mind
And quiet touch,
When my pounding heart
Is restless beating.

Autumn morning,
You ask too much for sure,
As your still mists linger long,
You bid me a few more hours endure,
When all my being is
Bursting now with song.

To Love

To love …
Is to mark the special time
Write lines that rhyme!
Reach heights sublime;

To love …
Is to salute all the dawns
Remember the prawns!
See magic in acorns;

To love …
To stroll among the trees
Gently tease!
Hear words on the breeze;

To love …
Is to hold trembling hands,
Skip to the bands!
Share footprints in wet sands;

To love …
Is to ache with deep longing,
Be oblivious to crowds thronging,
Know true belonging;

To love …
Is to catch a falling leaf
A hint of mischief,
Share deep belief:

To love
Is to share pain,
Have one umbrella in the rain!
Toast in champagne:

To love
Is to dream
Write ream after ream!
Cast roses in the stream:

To love …
Is to sigh deepest sighs,
Speak with the eyes:
Cry at goodbyes.

'Til Our Love

Life never so exciting
The distant hills never so inviting,
Nature's robes never so enchanting—
'Til our love.

Days never so awaited,
Journeys never so anticipated,
Feelings never so liberated—
'Til our love.

Memories never so full of reviving,
Moments never so often reliving,
Gifts never so sought for giving,
'Til our love.

A name never so adoringly uttered,
A soul never so joyfully related,
A heart never so completely devoted,
'Til our love.

'Thy Eternal Summer Shall Not Fade'

A borrowed line, but no matter what
Ancestor filled that poet's heart,
Penned for you, as all the tumblings
Out of joy, all the canvas visions,
And soaring notes, of all those who have
Loved, are for you, for in you is
Full beauty's art perfected,
Forever undimmed and nowhere surpassed;

All seasons offer their tidings to you
Nature sends trees to curtsey at your
Passing, birds to sweetly ripple the
Air around you, flowers to garland
Your path and scent your way;

No more can summer fade than
Earth be as sea, river become rainbow,
Or light be dark,
You are more beautiful with each dawn,
And noon and evening, and with each
Kiss more of paradise is known

Thoughts Provoked by a 'Blue' Mood

Imagine no going and no returning;
No parting wish,
No returning greeting—
It is monotony that kills, not change.
Imagine no urge to do, no striving,
No task that <u>has</u> to wait until another day.
Imagine arriving, once and for all,
No more map, no further road
Ending of unknowing, just here and no more,
We are not meant for a cul-de-sac,
For unmoving residence,
Imagine it all that was and what is now.
Fossils of feeling, stone imprisoned mood,
Frozen hope, replayed scene.
Imagine it all were still,
And no breeze,
If all were easy and no hard,
If all were straight and no bend,
If all were calm and no tug from some
As yet unlived experience.
Imagine—remember it's because we can
We know season's change,
Each dawns unrepeatable hues,
And that blue is the only colour.

There

There,
In that soundless place,
Before time was measured,
Our love began.

There,
When there was only love,
Our love was formed—
With patience, waiting.

There,
In shared time, growing nearness,
Our love was born
And took its wing.

There,
In knowing hearts,
In painful, joy-filled moments,
Our love shines.

There,
When all time ends,
And love completes its task,
Our love will be.

There Is

There is within the library of the
Mind,
A myriad of words, but nowhere can I
Find
The ones that sufficient blend to
Speak my love, to tell it's full,
Deep and deeper, yet, extent;
There is upon the palette of the
Eye,
A thousand tones but none
Supply
That perfect hue, no canvas rich
Enough in shades to display
The colours of my love:

There is within the register of the
Voice,
Countless notes but none of such
Choice
To sing the melody of my love, and all
The music of the ages touch, but
The beginning of the song.

There Is a Tree ...

There is a tree,
Rearing, rising,
Penetrating foliage,
That knows for ever
The tightening grip
Of lovers' limbs,
In a harmony of longing.

There is a tree,
Flecked with diamond leaves,
It's feet untidy with
Untrod brambles,
That, strong against all
Nature's surging
Now knows forever,
Even deeper passion,
Against its favoured bark.

There are paths,
Morning dewed,
Evening quiet,
That know forever
The echoes of tender words,
Love-led wandering feet,

Bursting hearts
Along their winding ways.
There is a wood,
Winter bare,
Summer coated,
That knows forever,
Within its secret heart,
The presence of
Undying love.

There Is a Gallery of Pictures in My Mind ...

There is a gallery of pictures in my mind,
Of many seasons, shades and hues,
Each of them with our twin imprint signed,
Intimate spots and wide spreading views;

Quiet, flower-scented country church is there,
Along with a mansion's mellowed calm
Laughter ringing 'round a London Square.
And corner teashops so full of charm.

Shrubs and plants with new learned names!
And some of which we could only guess.
And, favourite in the many of the lovely frames.
A robin, symbol of our togetherness;

Art's masterworks at which the heart thrills,
Roses cast on the Thames quick flow,
Honeyed stone 'twixt Cotswold hills,
Footprints in winter's new fall snow.

Whispered words in gracious hall,
Eager waves from a passing train,
A bridge by the pool of a waterfall,
A half-awake hamlet n a shower of rain:
All these and more so beautifully wove,
Memories alive in the head and the heart.
Milestones of our journey of love,
Our bond, our touch when we are apart.

The Journey of Our Love ...

Once as a mirage distant on the mind,
A glimpse of the infant rising sun,
Then a breeze and the first drops of summer rain,
Watering the smile that said I know.

Soon, flowers grew from the quickening pulse,
And thoughts and eyes one focus alone knew,
Then the fuller tide breeching
The waiting, now undefended walls,
And the joyous merging-miracle had shape.

The current long irresistible,
Harvest upon harvest calls
Where once a candle stood, now
A million suns
Where once a nervous hand,
Essays abound.

Where once dreaming hope, now
Eternal certainty,
Where once two, now, a forever one,
And the journey avenued
With beauty beyond word,
Has only just begun

The Heart

The heart
Explodes,
Bursting into body, mind and soul,
Pulsating love,
In human frame,
Deep contentment,
Urgent longing,
Blending,
Our love
Centre of the universe,
Sum of all love,
Yet
Birthplace of love waiting to be,
Giving pace to step,
Purpose to morning,
Words for the unspeakable,
Whispered words,
Eternally echoing
Lips,
Tenderly fusing,

Passionately seeking,
Marvellously finding,
Touch,
Turned to music

Sunlight Through a Window

On a day like today
This is not the place for you and me,
Caged, unable to find wing enough
To fly free, reach heights
Roam through all the unopened ways
The open heath, the expanse of shore,
The thickly carpeted woods,
The sunlit road,
These should be our habitat on
Such a day.

Some of My Favourite Things

Spoons for hot chocolate,
And flashing car headlights,
Walks by the river,
A phone call at midnight,
Notelets in bundles with me for each day,
With words of much love for while we're away,
When the night's long and the dawn's slow,
When I'm missing you, I get to
Recalling my favourite things and then
I don't feel so blue:
Mondays and Thursdays,
And Saturday's also,
Smoked salmon and picnics
And surprises brought for you,
Smiles in the mirror as we drive along
Tuned into melody and singing a song.
When the road bends and the view ends
And I'm missing you,
I get to recalling the moments before,
And that makes me feel more blue!

Poem Snippets of Love

Oh, thou art fairer than the evening air, clad in the beauty
Of a thousand stars

                                                  Christopher Marlowe

Grace was all in her steps,
Heaven in her eyes,

                                                  John Milton

But the loveliest things of beauty
God ever show to me,
And her voice, and her hair,
And eyes, and the dear red
Curve of her lips.

                                                  John Masefield

To kiss you, is to have a
Conversation with your heart.

                                                    Anon

If I could write the beauty of your eyes,
And in fresh numbers number all your
graces,
The age to come would say this poet lies,
Such heavenly touches
Nere touch earthly faces.

                                          William Shakespeare

Where you go,
I will go, and where you stay, I will stay.
Your people shall be my people,
And your God, my God. Where you die,
I will die, and there will I be buried.

                                              Ruth 1 v16–17

Love is the slipping of a hand
In another's, of knowing
Where you belong at last,
And of exchanging through the eyes
The all-consuming regard which ignores
Everybody else on earth.

                                                  Laurie Lee

Robin

Bold breasted friend,
Were you dispatched
From Creation's nest
With the one task.
To bless our love
With your presence?
Carrier of the smile
Of higher spheres,
Jewel-eyed witness to
The deepest love,
You link us when apart,
Like a garland,
With your dipping flight,
And signal with such
Lively call,
Our re-uniting.

Remembering

Slowly,
One house, and then another and low field walls,
Fractured here and there, began to mellow, turning
To dull honey softness,
Like a ripening, gentle on the eye;
Shy villages, hiding
Peeked above the folds of
Green and yet greener hills, keeping faith with the past;
The hard monument of Blenheim, it's precise and then Unkempt lawns,
White water licking smooth moss green rocks,
The last daffodils of a passing Spring, brown with dying, Ground hugging purple and soft yellow flowers,
Oak galls and vibrant ivy mimicking life in the husk
Of a once proud tree;
Poetry in a bus shelter!
Hamlets, quaintly named, still in the lazy air.
Lanes that only yesterday were avenues of a cart-slow world. Streams, lying peaceful by the road,

Busier Burton and cottages standing to attention climbing Burford's slope;
Then the wider road and quicker pace,
A different world

Behind the corners waiting to be turned.
Low bridged winding water, waiting to be crossed; Remembering, and echoes,
So many echoes!

Our Love

As brilliant as the jewels
Flung from the morning sun
Onto the waking lake;
As timeless as the most
Ancient hill;
As endless as the ever-deepening blue;
As tender as an opening flower;
As sweet as the first caress of cool water;
As strong as the most mighty oak;

....
our love.

Only You

If I could speak only one word,

It would be your name—

Hold only one thing,

It would be your hand—

See only one sight,

It would be your face—

Walk but one step,

It would be to your side—

Think only one thought—

It would be of you—

Hear only one sound,

It would be your word of love.

On Durlston Head
(Swanage)

The mist was unrelenting,
Grey in sky and sea
And matching stone.
The town, quiet, behind
Shuttered for cold months,
Summer's delight strangely
Uninviting:
Ahead, steeply up
Rising mounds of green downs,
To sudden edge of unattended cliff,
Below, the slow break
Of low tide on rounded rocks,
An unseen boat
Chugged towards
Hidden landing,
And in stillness,
A robin waited
Low on a bush
By the path
And in the silence, I spoke your name

Now I Know

Now I know
How time can be enemy and friend:
Enemy as it's ponderous steps refuse
To quicken to span the hours, the
Long days and nights,
When we're apart.
Friend, as, relenting, it bids the last
Hours dissolve into that
Beautiful moment of uniting.

Now I know
Why bright days blue and sun's
Unclouded face,
Can bring heartache,
For on such days as these
I want only to walk with you
Under blue sky's canopy,
Share with you,
From cool dawn's first ray
To eve's blood-orange slip
Beyond our sight,
The whole day's life.
Now I know
Why poet and painter
Make master works,
How with irresistible word and form
They can do no other,
For love takes pen and brush
And makes them extensions of the heart,
When in love, there is no mystery
That poem and scene,
Love's children are born.

Now I know
The oneness of heart and mind and soul,
As in you they find their home,
From you draw their strength,
With you, now contentment,
Now excitement know
In you forever reside.

Now I know.

No Single Bell

No single bell, or steeple full
With overflowing sound,
No petal-cup of rose, or
Stretching fields and chased buds,
No verse, or ream of prose,
No single chord, or
Full majestic symphony,
No one bright star, or arching,
Endless, galaxy,
No night, or day, nor all the
Different coloured seasons,
No single frame of beauty, nor
Every stroke of brush
Since time began,
No word, or the whole
Vocabulary of man,
Can speak, or show
The love I have for you.

Music and Fireworks

Above the sleeping house,
Mid between sodden earth and charcoal clouds,
A myriad colours danced, some burst,
Fragmented jewels umbrellaing the sky.
Others gently climbed and with slow step
Waltzed with the breeze, and fell
Extinguished, some crackled the night air,
And, once, a white waterfall sparkled.
Nature had held strange 'til then, splitting
The air in anger, fiery spears flung from
Horizon to horizon, and trees fiercely struggled
To take to the sky:
Waterproofed shapes passed to and fro,
Wellington shod or barefoot, uncaring of
The storm, the elements defied
For music's sake:
Welcome coffee, wine tipped with orange,
Dark-satined cherries, breeze-brought music:
So much remembered—and bright above all
You at my side, so gay, so lovely.

Memories

Now, with newly opened eyes,
Memories long stored, consciously
Or unknowing,
Are more precious still,
Overture to our
Mutual music now.

Memories—

Of gay laughter, infectious and free,
Echoing from many places
And times.
Of clever, funny rhymes, of perception
Woven in between that made them
True as well.

Memories—

Of care that found the one alone
In a crowded room and the time
Given to him or her.
Of when we partnered in Barn
Dance fun and my reluctant
Letting go to the one ahead!

Memories—

A time at a party when beauty
Stunned, and eyes that
Followed wherever you went
These and many more
That nothing will erase,
All part of an ever-richer tapestry
With unbelievable colours.

Meant to Be

A bird was made for sky,
As leaf for tree,
As fish for waters, deep,
So were we for each other born.

A river flows with rush or glide,
To waiting ocean,
As flower opens to warming sun,
So, we, with each other,
Are fulfilled,

As night holds circling hands
With day,
As rain renews,
As moon and stars share space,
So, we, together, belong

Love's Restlessness

A winter-spring sky,
Dimming shapes,
A quietening street,
No one else mattering,
Love and loveliness in my arms.

Growing thoughts,
Echoing, recalling
Precious hours,
Winged across time and space,
Helping close aching gap.

Restless, quivering, senses,
Longing for first sight,
Burning love,
Flamed again,
Transforming the day.
A myriad plans,
A million words,
A thirst beyond quenching
Until love and loveliness
Are in my arms again.

Love Is ...

Love,
'The many splendored thing'
Of song,
Merely dream,
Romantic,
But dream,
Until its splendours
Became real,
And overtake all else,
Influencing all else,
Infusing all else,
With meaning.

Love,
The tenderest, boldest,
Most momentous thing
Of all,
Thrill to body, mind,
And soul,
Holding captive
The hearts that love,
Yet releasing to
Know ever deepening
Joy
Without boundary or end.
Love,
That marvellous realm,
Of knowing and being
Known,
Of venture and of stillness,
Of giving and receiving,
The many splendored thing,
Running, bursting,
Through life,
With ever changing,
Ever swelling
Even richer,
Melody.

Love Is Fun

Love is fun!
It bubbles,
Sending waves
Around the heart,
Releasing the soul,
Cascading through the mind.

Love is fun!
Bringing smiles
To play upon the lips,
Sending shouts
Of joy, like a myriad smiling stars,
Flung against the night.

Love is fun!
Renewing youthful thrill,
Making children of
Our spirits,
Bouncing our steps
Like a rubber ball.

There is no laughter,
No greater mirth,
No humour so enchanting,
So intimate, so bright,
Than that of lovers,
Love is fun!

Love Has No Bounds

No ocean, white stirred by
Passing wind,
Can separate what is deeper
Than the deepest depths;

No sky, hazed or bright,
Clear or troubled by coming storm,
Dry, or weeping hard,
Can fail to cover both of us;

No clock or calendar,
However crawling in its speed,
Love has no bounds can ever stop, but has to yield
To that moment of reunion;

No silence can erase
Love's words, for they stay
Within the mind, and heart
And memory
And echo

Love has no bounds.

Longing

Like caged birds, wanting to be
Free to climb the heights for
Which they were made.
So, my love yearns
To lift us to realms beyond even
What we have known.

Like new sunlight slowly waking
Each shadowed place,
Filling it with ever stronger glow,
So, my love longs to give you,
Enfold you,
In its warmth.

Like the river's slow procession,
Lingering hold in its banks embrace,
So my love dreams of your
Unreleasing arms,
Holding each moment of my journey.

Like the perfect note of song
That answers need, confirms love,
So my love finds in you the
Pure chord heard when hearts

Meet and merge.
Like the first holy sip, after
Long thirst,
So my love is filled by your
Lip's deep, welcoming softness.

Like the spring flower,
Making icy grip yield,
So my love longs
To be for you,
At any winter time.

Let Them Not Spoil It

Let them not spoil it,
Our place of dreams and memories,
Let them not turn it into
A whim of modern mind,
Let them not make garish its
Gentle walls, nor hurt its
Silence with throbbing percussion sound;
Let them not break its spell
For want of popularity, not change
Its intimate shapes in search of
Regularity,
Let them not fret for stylistic floor,
But leave, untouched, the carpets tread,
Let leave alone the wise
And rising stair,
And the soaring ceiling overhead,
Let them not add fluorescent glow,
Nor change to hasty pace the service slow,
Let them not make it a foreign place,
But retain all its charm and lovely grace.

It's Poetry Day

Today they say
Is Poetry Day,
So the urge to satisfy,
I will versify!
I will write of apples,
Turning in the morning wind,
Green-red, ripening.
I will tell of autumnal sky,
With its own blue hue,
Not as summer or spring;
I will write of leaves,
Myriad tinted,
Red flamed or yellowing.
I will tell of the stillness
Creation's breath held
As if pondering,
But best of all things I write
Of my love for my love,
Ever new—never ending.

I Wish

I wish I was travelling West with you,
Without time's restraints,
To a land, over Severn's divide,
Of song and deep emotion
Of ancient cleavered valleys
Of breasted hills
I wish I was travelling West with you
In loving duet,
To show you beauty by nature,
Scars by man
To unforgettable places, to recount,
Relive, memories—for you.

I wish I was travelling West with you,
Unencumbered by others,
For the me of now to be in
Touch again,
With the me of then—for you.

I wish I was travelling West with you,
Enclosed in your love,
To places where legends
have easy birth and mystery
Reigns,
To places where tears would come and echoes be heard.
To share with you your first touch of this land, its
First touch of you.
I wish I was travelling West with you.

I Want to Walk with You

I want to walk with you,
Along a shore, 'neath purpled sky,
The only sounds, the soft gasp of playful waves,
The sigh of the sinking sun.

I want to walk with you,
High on hills, with crisp, cold wind for company, heather Catching at our feet, and a
Coverlet of fields below.

I want to walk with you
Beside a lake's still face, with flaming leaves carpeting air Path, shy creatures watching,
And autumn's glory all around.

I want to walk with you
Down wood-edged aisle, lit by stained glass windows glow Perfumed with faith, made
Beautiful by promises.

I want to walk with you,
Through falling snow, 'neath white wrapped boughs, With hanging breath, and footprints,
Showing the way we've come.

I want to walk with you,
Early, as earth, lightening, stretches herself awake,
A songbird fanfares the day
And the first breeze washes our face.

I Bring You a Rose

I bring you a rose,
A June rose
For your June day,
Velvet of petal,
Heady of scent,
Bright of glow—
I bring you a rose.

I bring you a heart,
A full heart
For your June day,
Endless of yearning,
Ceaseless of passion,
Deep of loving—
I bring you a heart.

I bring you a life,
A whole life,
For your June day,
Immeasurable of devotion,
Overflowing of blessing,
Timeless of adoring—
I bring you a life.

I Am with You

I am with you—

As the soft wind,

As the warming sun,

As the greener shoots,

As the morning air,

As the evening star,

As the beat of heart,

As the rest of sleep,

Are with you;

So am I with you!

I Love You

I love you—
Through every season of the year
I love you;
In spring with its fresh washed
Face calling the earth from
Winter rest, to play;
In summer, with its unmoving
Air, shimmering hills, and the
Sun staying warm, clinging to
The rim of the day;
In autumn, with its veils of
Mist, its golden gems tossed
From trees, and its early
Closing of the day;
In winter, with its nipping
Bite, its sullen hours, and
Its snowflakes in cold and
Windy play.
I love you

For You

I will be your anchor in storm,
Companion in pain,
Your shelter in tumult,
'til peace comes again.

I will be drink to your thirst,
Food for your hunger,
Sleep in your weariness,
Sharer of danger.

I will be your shade in the glare,
Your cool in the heat,
Your warmth in the winter,
And in sour your sweet.
I will be your silence in noise,
The tune for your song,
Bring reasons for laughter,
Your soft pillow the night long.

I will be your springtime and Christmas,
Your familiar and your new,
Your colour in drabness,
Your red, green and blue.
I will be there at dawning
And the close of the day,
There for life's journey,
Each step of the way.

For My Love ...

There's a wildness about my love for you,
That would sweep you off to pounding shore
Where surging, unstoppable tide
Would fill all, give all.
Quietening only slowly, to
Rise again as yearning and
Remembering met to send
Eager waves—higher, deeper still.

There's a stillness about my love
For you, that would stand content,
Rested with you. To hold you
In buffeting wind and shelter you in storm.
A stillness so real that words would break the spell.

There's a joy about my love for you,
Lifting high the soul as it blends with yours,
Finding in touch and being, harmony
And deep, deep melody.

There's a timelessness about my love
For you, its reservoir replenished
By all we share. Though hours
Press and days pass there is at

The deep heart of things a love
Time cannot touch.

For Ever I Am with You

I am with you—

As the soft wind,

As the warming sun,

As the greener shoots,

As the morning air,

As the evening star,

As the beat of heart,

As the rest of sleep,

Are with you;

So am I with you!

Creations of Love

Monet had his paintings,
Betjeman his rhyme,
Shakespeare had his sonnets,
Soft spoken for all time.

Lloyd Webber had his ballads,
The Beatles their song,
The musicals their melodies
To move the crowd that throng.

The writer has his tale to tell,
The artist his colour blends,
The poet has his magic words,
Each speaking of love that never ends.

Come all you creative spirits
Lend us your fullest art,
That I may show my dearest love,
All that lies within my heart

That beats with love profound,
And yearns only to share the joy,
Our blended lives have found.

Comes May

Comes May—

And rain falls soft,
Less cold,
The roses tint to Royal mantle shade,
And daisies dot the
Greening grass.

Comes May—

And blossoms fanfare
With clusters, soft against
The apple, cherry and the almond.
Tulips grow bold,
Dripping with
Fresh paint.

Comes May—

And ears fine tune
Again to shy borne music,
And summer's lively
Overture
Begins.

Comes May—

And all I see
Of beauty in its
Infinite forms,
Cannot compare with
Your loveliness and grace;
In form and soul
And face.

Come Words

Come, words
Come, give me some sounds
To speak the indescribable
Love that I feel.
Give me some shapes, to speak
What my bursting heart shouts
Each time we meet.

Help me frame more than the cry
That carries in its short
And single breath,
A whole eternity of longing.

Help me translate what I feel
When, in the still, still hours
Before dawn,
When the day is not yet born
From the womb of night,
I lie, wide-eyed,
Nothing stirring save my
Racing heart.
Help me give form to the
Love that bears me, to serene
Moments, in time with all things,
And help me graft from the agony
When apart,
What I need until we meet.
Come, words, come, with your long
Experience of other lovers' cries,
And provide for me an alphabet,
A language,
Or, just one new minted word,
Unheard before, that
Is mine alone,
To speak this love.

Come Take My Hand

Come,
Take my hand and
Let us stand
On the rim of the sea,
At our feet,
The sloping sand and the
Turning tide's retreat.

Come,
Hold my hand,
And, as one we see
The far horizon's edge,
Where wild clouds fly
And white topped waves break
To flood the sky.

Come,
Take my hand in yours
And let the touch
Bind and blend our love,
Love as wide and deep as all we see
From ocean's shore,
More lovely in its harmony.

Come

Come walk with me in days of long ago,
Step back in time to a gentle way,
When hours stretched, and sun lingered over
The day's Amen, the moon played with stars.
Visible to view, and a quiet, living stillness
Settled with lullaby and light to sleep.

Come, to a place, a water-cressed stream,
Flitting dragon flies, and the glinting
Sun glossing the unhurrying water, now
Pausing beneath the arch of a
Hewn-wood bridge.

Come to a scene that wakes the memory,
The solitary gardener at dusk, the horse
In the fence-ringed field, free of the
Dray, the courting coo of pigeons in the
High trees of the wood, the hearths of
Houses lit, one by one, at twilights
Bidding, the roosting birds, the
Speckled sky, and a shadowy cat abroad.

Come, to a dawn, to a morning breathing
Deep before the day, a pale orange sun,
Milkman and postman meeting, as every day,
By the high rust wall, a dog, more friend
Than foe testing the unmoving air,
Then, as if with giant spoon a breeze
Stirs the trees, and like a play begun,
The calendar so slowly turns once more.

Christmas Joy

Christmas joy be yours, my love

In the echoes from your childhood time,
In majesty of carol's rhyme,
In trees and houses with lights ablaze,
In all the excitement of a child's gaze,
In the retelling of the familiar story,
In the sharing of angelic glory,
In the thrill in each other we've found,
In our love, deep, beautiful and profound.

Christmas peace be yours, my love,

In the still earth of winter white
In the rhythm of distant geese's flight,
In the holy moments of unspoken prayer,
In the sound of bells borne on frosty air,
In the hush of late evening's hour,
In the loveliness of a favourite flower,
In the hardly moving candle flame,
In my quiet speaking of your name.
Christmas love be yours, my love,
In your smile as you dress in seasonal red,
In the sound of a toast from a distance said,
In all the meaning of a stable birth,
In God's clear imprint on this needy earth,
In the sight of our red-breasted friend,
In my presence with you at this day's end,
In our togetherness each step of the way,
In our hearts and souls on this Christmas Day.

Born in June

Born between the longest day,
And Midsummer Day,
When the year is at its height,
The sun on its furthest span,
The earth in bloom, and
Nature in summer clothes,
Is how it should be for
One so lovely,
So tuned to nature's gifts,
So full of grace,
For one in whom such
Beauty dwells that at her glance
Flowers yield more beauty still,
And find new creation in her touch,
This, this June, is the season
Of your birth, as from the
Centre of the year you came,
There could have been no better time
For one so lovely to be born.

Because of You

There is no ordinary sky,
No ordinary view,
No ordinary street, or vale or hill,
Because of you …

There is no ordinary day,
No ordinary colour blue,
No ordinary flower, or leaf or rain,
Because of you …

There is no ordinary sound,
No ordinary night time dew.
No ordinary moon or star or sun,
Because of you …

There is no ordinary tree,
No ordinary avenue,
No ordinary picture, song or verse,
Because of you …

There is no ordinary love,
No ordinary yearning too,
No ordinary truth or touch or smile,
Because of you.

And I Think of You ...

Autumn's rising tide
Laps at summer's warming shore
And I think of you.

The morning sun wakes to cloudless sky,
A tree makes patterns on September grass
And I think of you.

Bees linger over summer's first sweetness.
Apples with blushing cheeks await the hand,
And I think of you.

Leaves begin to dress in autumn fashion,
Hints of mist greet the day,
And I think of you.

At each clock finger's turn,
Through each day's course,
In every season's mood,
I think of you

And I Love You

In rain or sun
On riverbank or town street,
In light or shade,
I love you.

When spirits sink and
Heart's turmoil mounts
When questions rise and
Lurk unanswerable,
I love you.

Alone or in crowds,
Together or apart
Holding you or
Dreaming of you,
I love you.

When the step is light and
The spirit soars
When we are at peace inside
I love you.

When love's craving
Finds expression and
Gentle touch,
Excites or calms,
I love you.
When days are long and calendar, unfeeling,
Mocks our need,
When time relents and
Waiting love fires again
I love you.

An Invitation

There are places deep in Surrey,
Beckoning,
Shere, it's streamside walk,
Gomshall, it's mill.
It's fascinating shop,
High Leith Hill,
Friday Street, Nestling in its hollow,
As if undiscovered.
Abinger, its hammer poised,
Silent pool of ancient tale.
Full of mystery,
Tall tree forests,
Sudden views 'cross mist
Filled valleys,
Shadow filled lanes,
High banked,
There are places deep in Surrey,
Beckoning,
Calling my love and I.

An Anniversary—
The Days of All These Years

The days of all these years,
Each with echo sweet upon the mind,
Lit, lit, and still brighter lit,
By ripening love,
Fragranced with sharing, knowing,
Thrill and peaceful times,
The days of all these years;

Then days of all these years
Are not without their pain,
Arrowheads stab at parting and ache,
More than human bearing,
Of longing, needing, yearning,
Brings the heart to weeping,
On each day of all these years;

Through the days of all these years,
I have not heard in fact
Nor in story told,

From ancient nor from modern time,
Words with more feeling filled nor
More deeply born,
Out of the days of all these years;
In the days of all these years,
Through touch, kiss, and through
Meeting eyes,
I have drunk at love's eternal spring,
And felt the brush of angelic wing,
And found my soul's, my heart's,
My own, home,
For all the days of all the years to be;

How tell the words that shape give
To all I feel?
How speak the overflowing heart
That your beauty, your grace, has awakened?
How, with only mortal sounds, unlock
The tongue and voice all, all,
Of the days of all these years;

The days of all these years—
How tell their bliss?
This, this
I do, as I have done through
Every hour of all these years,
Send on transporting air
My calling of your name, and
From the deeps of heart and soul,
Speak the words that are ours,
Only loaned to others,
'I love you',
And my devotion give,
For the days of all the years to be.

After Summer Rain

The roses still weep,
Close-cupped heads shedding quiet tears
Fallen apples, small, hard with
Unripeness, lie at the feet of their host;
The tree's branches bowing
Constantly to a stream of
Unseen monarchy;
The grass is greener,
Pavements dry in patchwork,
And wooded bench
Where raindrops with
Bouncing silver skirts had danced,
Has wisps of steam as if
On smouldering fire.

Birds are on the move again,
A cat creeps low from the dripping hedge,
Fur slicked tight.
Car tyres hiss at each other like
Disturbed snakes.
Here and there windows open again,
And a child hurriedly called in,
Returns to his outside game.
The sky lightens,
A slow wash of grey stained clothes,
A moist sun comes and goes,
Heralding a rainbow.
One lagging cloud grieves openly,
Briefly bringing an eruption
Of still wet umbrellas,
The darker soil welcomes
The thirsty leaves leftover rain,
And a soft towel of warm air
Dries the rose's tears.

After Our Meeting

I am not here,
In this place, this
Hollow place of sighs,
This place of pacing
To and for,
I am not here.

I am there,
In that sun-drenched place,
Where two of us belong,
Where all that is of beauty
Has home,
Where every sound
Is wrapped in love, and every
Touch a message tells.

I am not here,
I am there, where
Though outside intrudes
It cannot break the spell

Woven by beating,
Yearning hearts.
By passion high,
By calm and gentle holding.

I am not here,
Except this shell,
I am there,
With you my love,
Wherever you are.

A 'Midsummer Night's Dream'

I know a place
Where dust-grey paths,
Crevice cracked,
Led to tall grasses
And beyond, a quiet river.
A place where the sun,
High in pale mauve sky,
Melted the distant views
Into haze of green.

I know a place
Where waking came
New summer-coated,
Welcomed, beckoned,
As if made ready
A place of love
Of deep-welled kisses,
Of tender words,
And the warm earth for witness.

I know a place …

A Special Place

It has taken us into its intimate heart,
And we made of it our secret place
Of dreams and quiet conversation,
Of peace and smiling love;
Its doors have opened for us
In all seasons—Winter's footprints
Left outside to fill with falling snow,
Spring's shadows playing
Games across the lawn,
The heatless hearth in summer
Has hosted melting logs of flame
On cooler days;
Now and again half opened doors
Have teased with more delights,
Wide stairs asked to be climbed,
Once, with disappointed laughter, we found
Taped tunes and no pianist to hear
Whispered request!
There enclosed in cosy walls,
We are alone, no matter that

Others come and go,
If they notice they may
See or sense our love,
For each other and
For this special place.

A Time Apart (1)

The opening of your card
Each morning, quiet and before
The day,
Moments of pain
And joy,
Of smile and tear,
Each lovely bead
Strung across the waiting time.

A Time Apart (2)

How tell the heart's pain?
How speak the weeping within?
How form the shape of loneliness?
How frame the longing of the soul?
How write the bodies ache?
How show the restless mind?
I, nor any other, have words
To give to these,
They cannot be expressed,
They are endured,
Searing,
Breaking me apart.

A Special Place

Darkened lane,

High hedged and set apart

From traffics flow,

Island paradise,

Place of togetherness,

For all too brief a time,

Made ours by,

Our love's mark on this

Corner of the world

A Robin Sang

(With apologies to that nightingale that sang in Berkley Square)

That day in June when you were born,
I'm perfectly willing to swear,
That with the hush that came with dawn,
A robin sang in the sunlit air;

The days may come, the days may go,
But of this I am so fully aware,
That when we meet and say hello,
A robin sings in the sunlit air;

To you my love, I want to say,
Here's all my love and care,
And for you this day, this special day,
A robin will sing in the sunlit air;

And so we go, my dearest dear,
With all the future to share,
And this we'll know forever near,
The robin's song on the sunlit air.

A Morning in London

Each scene is etched so clear,
The multi-pictured wall,
Quiet compositions of
Green and blue, pale in their
Watery art;
The designs, modern yet with appeal
And not out of place as some
We've seen;
The cafe, almost to ourselves, until
Full orchestral sound beats the air,
And our words, submissive:
The walk by a cold slate lake, and
Land and water birds looking only,
For food, parting as we passed;
And 'St Francis' in St James Park,
Still as a tree, holding seed for
Sparrows, light and in the air,
Pigeons, heavier, beneath his feet,
And a single squirrel making timid
Scampering runs, tail raised like
A rudder against the wind;
His eyes met ours and in his hand
Invited us to join his communion
With the birds … and the sparrows came
To stand like fragile twigs, upon
Our hand;
Side by side we fed them until the
Last few seeds fell between our fingers.

A Gift of a Snowdrop

Snow white, snowdrop,
Fragile herald of
Coming spring,
Newly flowered,
Plucked with
Loving hand, a gift
Of two-fold beauty—
That which lies within
The slender green and
Unblemished white of
Stem and bell,
And the beauty of the love
That lies within the choice,
And thought,
And bringing.

A Few of My Favourite Things

The love in your kiss
Your body's grace
Your shy eyes
Your soft voice on the telephone
The touch of our souls
Your joy in flowers
The dip of your head as you run
Your relaxed body against mine
My first sight of you when we've been apart
The racing pulse before I ring you
Your hand in mine
The thrill of falling for you each time we meet

A Country Church Remembered

The sun bright, hot in the mid-morning sky,
Respected the sanctity and stayed beyond the studded door,
Within, cool reverence and dim light from narrowed glass,
No flowers, which last time tumbled all around,
Save one vase, remembering the Sunday past.
Soft hassocked step, and, for a moment, through
The yielding cloth, a touch of stone on the bending knee. Altar rail for resting arms, and in the calm cool silence Words came, filling the mind from time before,
As if fresh voiced now,
And new words softly uttered, from the surrendered heart. Rose, cradled for a moment on the holy air,
Becoming one with ancient walls, and then released
For their gentle journey to your inner hearing.
Outside all was held in the grip of the zenith seeking sun, And the door closed, slowly on the place,
Not only of memory,
But of meaning to.

A Christmas Apart

Under greying skies,
Beside the great house,
Quiet, save for brief birdsong
Still in the December air,
A garden.

Under sloping timber beams,
A triangle of rust red brick
And darkened honey wood,
Slatted—and long weather-hardened—
A bench.

A place of gifts,
There, as on Christmas dawn,
Gifts were shared,
Assembled in love,
Bearing love.

Under high, pale ceiling,
In a room of
Age-past grace,
Warmed by open fire,
Peace in loving.
A time of gifts,
A place of gifts,
And for each other
The gift above all gifts, Love.

A Rose

I took the rose,
To the park's distant edge,
And laid it with a kiss,
Cushioned by an ancient tree.

A tree that has stood
'Gainst wind and storm,
And seen time come and go,
And remained like our love.

I turned and looked across
To other trees,
Waist deep in green fern,
Each, in gentle breeze,
Nodding approval of my choice.

I stayed a while,
Silent with memories of other roses,
As pain and peace
Mingled, inside.

I turned again to that rose,
Remembering,
The eyes that chose it,
The love that gave it.
And with sighs of joy and longing
Remembered the moment
Of gifts,
Of slender coil,
Of full bloom flower.

And lived again,
The rapture, the sharing,
And saw again,
The loveliness beyond dream,
Beyond compare.

A July Morning

The unhurried river, slowly melting on each shore,
Boats in anchored line, swaying in time to gentle currents flow
And above a flamed blue sky.

A summer's day
Paths, one river following,
The other bending to greet the common's edge,
Swelling mounds, wild grassed
And below a bed of green.

A noon time,
A bench shaded by tall trees,
A long draught of twinned devotion, of purest joys
Slowly drink,
And around, the perfect air of love.

Whence the Poet in Me?

Whence the poet in me?
From remembered, unremembered,
Seeds, sown, scattered, on the infant,
Fertile, unknowing, field of tender time?

Whence the rhyme?
From some melody of sounds and shapes,
That played gently on the listening,
On the hearing without the name?

Whence the need, the longing, the
Unquenchable need to say, to speak,
To pen, to tell?
Ah! That is easier—joyfully so—
It is you, my love, answer and arouser.

Whence the liberty, the release, the
Recipient, of all that unbidden lay,
'til now?
That too is you—
My love.

I Long for You

Everywhere is quiet, the silence loud upon my ears,
As the day disappears, and
I long for you.

Everything is still, my heart, beating
With the passing of the day, the only
Motion visible, and
I long for you,
My thoughts echo, echo, with your voice.

Everything sleeps it seems, goodnights
Are said as the day turns off
It beams, and I long for you,
And all my yearnings hold no ease.

Everywhere holds breath, poised for the
New day's silent tread
Upon the earth, and
I long for you,
And myriad sighs cross the bridge of sleep.
And I long for you

Has There Ever Been a Time

Has there ever been a time
When I have not loved you?
Was it not there at the dawn of time
This seed now with such beautiful bloom?
Was it not there
Before we knew, looked, spoke
And found this deepest of all things?
Waiting to be uncovered, unlocked,
Always in ready soil
But needing fertile blending of each other
To come to birth?
Has our kiss not been rehearsed in our dreams,
Our words mouthed
In the silence of the night,
Our touching and holding been felt in
Our innermost core?
All before we knew, breathlessly
That it could be.
Have not our words found new shape—
All of them now with pregnant meaning,

Not a single one without its message?
All earlier words, prelude.
Knowing now, this too we know.
This love comes not from shallow ground and
It will not die.

Commonplace Made Special

Bookshop,
Shelved witness,
To our meeting,
Surrounded by words,
Our love is conveyed
By eyes and touch,
'Though only minutes apart,
I am enraptured again
By the thrill of meeting.

Cafe
And coffee
Ordinary,
But your radiance
Transforms it to a place
Of beauty and memory.
Hands clasped
In corner seat—
Another spot of heaven.

Rain
And an umbrella,
Unremarkable,
Yet close to you
My heart beats,
And bounds for joy
As our love makes the
The commonplace
Special

A Country House Hotel

Its very name beckons—
Conjuring to mind Latin warmth,
Grapes falling like ribbons
From balconies, arcs of
Sea-edged sand, skies of Italian
Blue, and melodic voices,
Tones of love;

Grace is there, in air and pillar,
Fire surround and wide rising stair,
Often it is still, as if another time
Is captured, and even in activity
There is a seated island, fringed
With passing waves of occupied lives;

A place that welcomes, independent
Of human greeting, it is as if
It smiles, and rises as we approach,
And we are with a friend,
Sharer of our love and soft uttered
Words, of our laughter and moist eyes,
One day, one eve, it will enclose
Us in its upper arms, and from
Below will come the accompanying
Music of the warm night.